HE KNOWS, YOU KNOW

50p

BOBCAT
BOOKS

LONDON/NEW YORK/SYDNEY/COLOGNE

© 1985 Bobcat Books
(A Division of Book Sales Limited)

Edited by Chris Charlesworth
Art Direction by Mike Bell
Book Designed by Mainartery
Picture research by Valerie Boyd
Typeset by TPP Limited
Printed by Blantyre Printing &
Binding Limited, Blantyre,
Glasgow

ISBN: 0.7119.0768.4
Order No: OP 43512

Exclusive Distributors:
Book Sales Limited,
78 Newman Street,
London W1P 3LA, UK.

Omnibus Press,
GPO Box 3304, Sydney,
NSW 2001,
Australia.

Cherry Lane Books,
PO Box 430,
Port Chester, NY 10573, USA.

To the Music Trade only:
Music Sales Limited,
78 Newman Street,
London W1P 3LA, UK.

Picture credits:
London Features International
Limited, Jon Blackmore, Barry
Plummer, Joe Bangay, Justin Thomas.

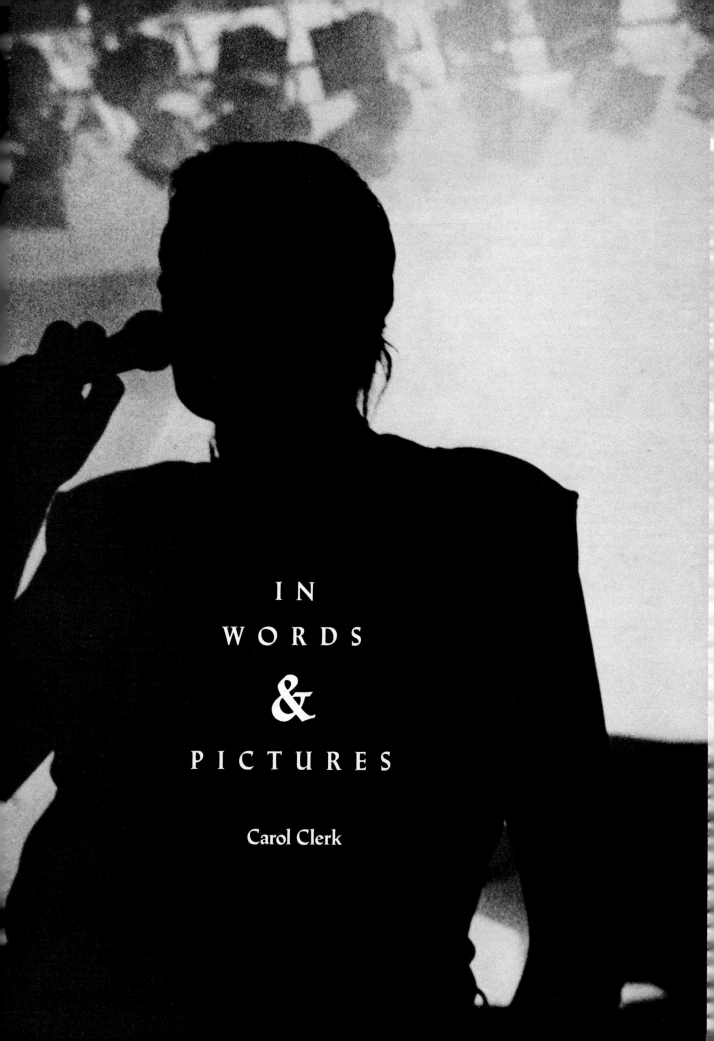

IN
WORDS
&
PICTURES

Carol Clerk

It was early, very early, in 1983, and the setting was a cellar bar in Wardour Street, London – just across the road from the Marquee and a few steps further along towards Oxford Street.

Then, as now, the St Moritz liked to think of itself as a "club". You did, admittedly, need a membership card to get in, but really, this was little more than a late-night drinking den and a favourite meeting place for musicians. There were all sorts here, a colourful assortment of punks and glam-rockers and heavy metal ruffians with one thing in common: a grip on reality.

The St Moritz clientèle shared a genuine distaste for the trendy nightspots of the West End – you know, the sort that look you up and down before they let you through the doors, bombard you with laser shows, drown out any potential conversation with music from which there's no escape, charge a fortune for ridiculous cocktails and go to any length, *every* length, to be more bizarre and outrageous than the next pleasure dome around the corner.

In the St Moritz, you made your own entertainment. If you wanted music, well, there was a disco of sorts. If you didn't, then you only had to stroll back out to the centre bar and through another doorway into the side room or one of its hideaway cubby-holes where you could decently hear your own voice amid the hearty babble of many others. Pride of place belonged to the big, round, wooden table accommodated in a cove in the wall.

People gathered in the St Moritz to drink, chat, maybe have a party and maybe not, enjoy the very lack of facilities, organisation and fussy furnishing. The nearest you got to a carpet in here was a bed of old fag ends, smouldering on the concrete. On any given night, you might expect to find Lemmy jangling furiously at the fruit machine, Bananarama trying out a few new steps on the microscopic dance floor, or Max Splodge conducting his usual ludicrous participation games at the round table. Helen Terry and her mates were no strangers to the St Moritz. Nor were Jake Burns, Beki Bondage and Rock Goddess, Chelsea, Terraplane and Hanoi Rocks. Nor was Fish.

Marillion, at the time, were in residence at the Marquee studios, working on their début album, "Script For A Jester's Tear". And Fish, who's not averse to a dram or ten at the end of a hard night's work, had set up a second home in the St Moritz. His towering figure at the bar, dwarfing the deliberately undernourished bodies of the rock 'n' rollers who flocked around him, was one of the most familiar and memorable images of the club in that era.

Everybody loved Fish – everybody except for a handful of idiots whose extreme inanity would be rewarded by a swift and scathing dismissal. Outside of such moments, Fish was splendid company, a fund of amusing anecdotes and cheerful quips. In the much later hours, though, when the laughter had subsided and half the revellers were either throwing up or passing out, Fish would choose his company and settle down for a serious discussion.

Fish would talk for hours about anything and everything, although, inevitably, he would return to his two great preoccupations: the world around us and the world within us. Current affairs, and affairs of the heart. These, of course, have always been his over-riding concerns as a lyricist.

Several things were compelling, fascinating, about Fish. One was his determination to explain himself to any relative stranger in the most astonishing personal detail. Another was his intensity, eyes fixed on his listener, demanding your attention through every stage of the conversation, making you not only understand but *feel* his points of view. The third was his notebook.

Fish would waste no opportunity to open up the battered old exercise book, crammed full of ideas, images and poems (many of which would later materialise as Marillion lyrics) and quote extensively from it to illustrate his particular lines of argument.

Clearly, Fish was not a man who merely *played* with words and lyrics. He was a man with an urgent compulsion to express in writing his most intimate and important feelings. The lyrics, it was obvious, were the man, and the man the lyrics.

Fish would talk of Marillion, their function, their capabilities, their future, with the same obsessive conviction.

Whatever he predicted, you'd generally agree with, not because he was six feet five and Scottish, but because there was something *unstoppable* about him. Marillion had even then confounded their critics by selling out the London Hammersmith Odeon – having previously released only one single. A second night had subsequently been added and that, too, had sold out.

However, there was still a great deal more to prove. There was much talk in the music press of a "progressive rock revival" with Marillion at the helm, but Fish would not tolerate the idea of Marillion as the leaders of any mere cult or fad. The group, he insisted time and again, would sweep the board, would reach the fans of Haircut 100 as well as Headbanger 100, would accept no boundaries or barriers, and would do this without any sacrifice of the essence or integrity of their music.

It was in January '84, with the release of "Punch And Judy", that Marillion first demonstrated their capacity to reach a young, pop-orientated audience. The single, with its captivating melodies and rhythmic ingenuity, was unlucky to travel no higher than 25 in the charts.

However, 1985 has justified all of Fish's early-morning prophecies at the round table. A number two single with "Kayleigh" and a number one album with "Misplaced Childhood", Marillion's finest work to date, have served to silence the more spiteful of their observers... people like Robert Godfrey of The Enid who revealed himself as a man of great perception and intelligence in the summer of '83 when he proclaimed that Marillion "will assuredly be on the scrapheap within two years".

I hope he's choking on his words.

The story begins in Aylesbury, Bucks, at Christmas, 1978, when drummer Mick Pointer formed a four-piece instrumental group called Silmarillion – named after the book by "Lord Of The Rings" author J.R. Tolkein. After only one gig, the guitarist left, and the band advertised in the music press for a replacement.

One Sunday morning in the summer of '79, Steve Rothery arrived unannounced from Whitby, Yorkshire, and walked into the job. Steve, born on November 25, 1959, in Brampton, South Yorkshire, was a self-taught musician who'd previously played with a series of school bands.

A local keyboard player came into the line-up in August, and Silmarillion finally began to take shape. They played their first gig at Berkhamsted Civic Centre on March 1, 1980, to a less than ecstatic response from the crowd. Undeterred, they agreed on a policy of taking every gig that was going, and chalked up a further 13 dates.

The line-up changed yet again in November with the departure of the bass player. The group, by this time, had decided to recruit a vocalist, so both vacancies were advertised in **Melody Maker.** Mick and Steve were particularly interested in one call from a couple of chaps in Scotland and duly sent the applicants a tape of "The Web" (instrumental). Enter Fish!

He arrived in Aylesbury several days later with all his luggage, a complete set of lyrics for "The Web" and a bassist called Diz Minnitt.

Fish, born Derek William Dick on April 25, 1958, in Dalkeith, near Edinburgh, worked his way through a variety of small and unsatisfying bands and an even larger number of unsatisfying jobs: a garage attendant, a student with the Forestry Commission, a tree surgeon, a dole office deskman and a quality inspector for garden sprinklers!

Marillion, who by now had dropped the "Sil", were pleased to offer the former lumberjack and his mate Diz the vacant positions in the band. They went into rehearsals straight away and played their first gig at the Bicester Red Lion on March 14, 1981. They soon came to the attention of a character called David Stopps, manager of the Aylesbury Friars venue, who booked them as support to John Cooper Clarke during Aylesbury Arts Week in May and helped arrange more dates on their behalf.

Marillion spent part of the summer recording a demo tape which they sent to promoters all over the country and also sold at gigs. It contained "He Knows, You Know", "Garden Party" and "Charting The Single".

In the second half of 1981, they gigged relentlessly. They hired London public relations consultant Keith Goodwin to service the press with details of their activities and played around 100 dates, supporting such diverse talents as Lindisfarne and Budgie, John Martyn and Girl. They had already built up a considerable and loyal following by the time the keyboard player left and was succeeded, in November, by Mark Kelly.

Mark, born on April 9, 1961, in Dublin, taught himself to play on a Hammond organ which he bought at the age of 15. By then, he'd moved to Romford with his parents. Eventually he became involved with a number of local bands including Chemical Alice – and it was at one gig with Chemical Alice that he made a striking impression on the support band: Marillion. When the keyboard vacancy arose, Mark was remembered and invited to join.

And it was around this time that Marillion really began to start moving.

They played their first gig of 1982 supporting Spider at the London Marquee and were booked back for the first of many headline dates on January 25. The media, by now, were finally starting to pay attention to Marillion, impressed by the strength of their following, intrigued by the character of Fish with his mask make-up and theatrics, interested in the scope and colour of the music and lyrics.

A radio session on Tommy Vance's Friday Rock Show was broadcast on February 26. It featured "The Web", "Three Boats Down From The Candy" and "Forgotten Sons". **Sounds** and **Kerrang!** ran enthusiastic features. And public demand for information on the group led to the setting up of the Marillion newsletter, **The Web.**

However, the line-up was still on the shaky side. Diz Minnitt left in March, and auditions for a replacement led to the recruitment of Pete Trewavas.

Pete, born on January 15, 1959, in Middlesborough, moved to Aylesbury at the age of six. He took up guitar a year later, switching to bass when he formed his first band at 12. He then moved through a succession of local groups, eventually settling with the Metros and, finally, Marillion. It was something of a baptism by fire for Pete. He was given only two weeks to learn the set before a 25-date tour of Scotland, arranged by Fish.

By the end of the summer Marillion had played a string of Marquee headlines and made history by becoming the first unsigned band to top the bill at Aylesbury Friars. August brought appearances at the Theakston and Reading festivals, more press for the clippings file and a fiercely-fought battle amongst the major record companies, all of them anxious to secure the Marillion signatures.

In September Marillion signed a world-wide recording contract with EMI Records.

Work began immediately. On October 25 Marillion released their debut single, the tuneful and pacey "Market Square Heroes" – a warning against "front room politicians" and an indictment of the human tendency to follow leaders. "Three Boats Down From The Candy" appeared on the B-side, and the 12″ version additionally featured a 17-minute epic, the extraordinary "Grendel", an established live favourite.

Grendel, in case you're wondering, is the name of the big green monster in the poem "Beowulf". (There is, in the Marillion camp, another big green monster to contend with. It's the band cocktail, an absurdly potent mixture of rum, vodka, Advocaat, Blue Bols, Crème De Menthe, Cointreau, cream and lemonade. Affectionately dubbed a Grendel, this drink has been known to do strange things to the band and especially to their manager John Arnison who has, under its influence, performed a rivetting series of impersonations of David Bellamy).

The single was released to mixed reactions from the press, and the band set off on a month-long UK tour to promote it. The tour culminated with a hastily arranged date at the prestigious London Venue. It sold out. And the single finally peaked at number 60.

In December Marillion went into the Marquee studios with producer Nick Tauber to record their début album "Script For A Jester's Tear", breaking only for three Christmas dates at the Marquee club. This made a total of 4 headline shows at the Marquee in 1982.

Only two items of news were heard from the studio-bound Marillion during the first two months of 1983. The first was the announcement of a full-scale British spring tour, climaxing at the London Hammersmith Odeon. The second was the release of their second single, "He Knows, You Know" c/w "Charting The Single", with the full-length album version of "He Knows, You Know" on the 12″ version.

The April 17 Hammersmith date sold out straight away, and another added night, on the 18th, did the same thing. The single was released on January 31. Again, the reviews in the music press were varied, but the public was becoming even more convinced; it reached number 35. And at the same time, Marillion were voted "Best New Band" in the **Sounds** readers' poll.

The tour was an enormous success. People flocked to the gigs, as they did to the autograph-signing sessions which were set up in record stores in every town. The Reading concert marked the last gig by any group in the town's Top Rank. And amongst other memorable performances, the second night at Hammersmith was filmed for a video, "Recital Of The Script", which was released in October of that year.

The album, meanwhile, was proving a spectacular success. "Script For A Jester's Tear", released on March 14, went shooting into the charts at number seven. The six-track LP attracted excellent reviews from most of the major music papers. It also laid Marillion's cards full out on the table.

Musically, "Script" is a drama, its arrangements, melodies, lights and shades and atmospheres moving one into another with authority and all of the polished, yet often dangerously edgy, musicianship that Marillion had always promised. Mark and Steve, the men responsible for the music (with help from Pete on arrangements), use keyboards and guitar to build upon the very definite scene-setting by the rhythm section.

These six tracks, and the contrasting passages within them, are pictures in music, the same pictures that Fish is simultaneously providing in words with his lyrics. Working together, the sound and the textures and the text lead the listener through a whole gallery of emotions, a burst of

As a writer, Fish favours the poetic approach. He's fond of using symbols, like the jester, for instance, and he actually thinks in images, romantic and otherwise, traditionally attractive or uncomfortably direct. For every "tinsel angel and perfumed child", there's the "blank eyes, purple fever" of a junkie, or the vision of "just another coffin on its way down the emerald aisle". Fish has never been, by any means, a comforting lyricist. Even the "tinsel angel" ends up topping herself.

"Script" is a collection of stories, each with its own character in a certain situation in a succession of certain moods. It sets a precedent which Fish has followed ever since: that is, he approaches the subject matter in the context of his own emotional state of mind. That state of mind will influence the angles of his "love themes", and it will underlie his explorations in other areas. The personal investigations of this album involve the gradual decline of a relationship after the first euphoric vows of love have been exchanged, the final incompatibility of the original soulmates.

"Can you still say that you love me?" he inquires dramatically on the title track. The answer, of course, is in the same song: "Too late to say I love you/Too late to restage the play/The game is over".

There's little joy in the heart of the lonely bedsit character in "The Web", only a brave optimism towards the end of the track. The web itself, another of Marillion's symbols and one which has often appeared as part of the stage set, represents the means by which people try to avoid making difficult decisions. This is a reference to the legend of Ulysses' wife Penelope, whom he deserted. When his father, the King, died and Penelope became the Queen Regent, she set about weaving a shroud for him.

As Fish says: "Everybody wanted to marry her, but she was so in love with Ulysses that she put off the decision. She said she'd make it when she'd woven the shroud, but she never finished it, never had to make the decision".

Wherever the webs are, for Marillion there are always windows – another familiar stage feature: "It's like people standing outside windows, deciding whether or not to go through. It's as if the webs are the questions and physical movement through the window is actually the decision. What Marillion try to do is provide the windows, make people aware, make people think".

Elsewhere on "Script", Fish takes on the subject of drug abuse and reactions to it ("He Knows, You Know"), a clever and amusing, if bitter, dig at the Cambridge mentality ("Garden Party"), the superficial life and useless death of a Kings Road dolly bird ("Chelsea Monday"), and the waste of human life in Northern Ireland (the chilling "Forgotten Sons").

Marillion may provide the soundtrack, point to the webs, show you the windows, but Fish will not offer any answers: That's *your* job!

Immediately after the 1983 March/April tour of Britain, drummer and founder member Mick Pointer was sacked from the band due to "musical incompatibility". In the early summer, he was replaced by Andy Ward, a founder member of Camel.

Andy made his live début with the band at a special garden party concert at Stowe Public School in Buckinghamshire, and also appeared with Marillion when they played the Marquee under the name of "Skyline Drifters" during the club's 25th anniversary celebrations.

On June 6 Marillion's third single, "Garden Party", was released. Its B-side was a live version of "Margaret" – a re-working of an old favourite Scottish traditional tune. The 12" version contained the full-length "Garden Party", a 13-minute version of "Margaret" and a live version of "Charting The Single" recorded at Hammersmith Odeon. The single reached number 16, taking Marillion on to "Top Of The Pops" for the first time.

It was also in the month of June that Marillion gave their first public airing of material from the next album. Audiences at the Glastonbury CND festival on June 17 were given a preview of the powerful "Assassing". They accorded it a suitable response. The band, right after Glastonbury, flew off for a five week tour of America and Canada, but came back earlier than expected after sacking yet another drummer.

Fish was unwilling to talk at any length about the dispute between the group and Andy Ward. He simply said: "It was due to personal reasons which I don't want to go into. Us and Andy saw that it wasn't working out, so we called the tour to a halt and came home".

John Martyr, drummer with Bernie Marsden's SOS,
stood in with the band for their Reading Festival
appearance on August Bank Holiday Saturday, although
Andy Ward, who'd been looking forward to the gig, was
invited to join in on extra percussion as a favour.
Certainly, this was one of Marillion's most remarkable gigs.
They gave a thrilling show, theatrically gripping and
musically dynamic. In terms of both performance and
crowd response, they wiped the floor with the headliners,
Black Sabbath. The day, decisively, belonged to Marillion.

In October the band announced that the new drummer would be Jonathan Mover whom they'd met in New York during a five-day support tour with Rush. True to his name, however, Jonathan moved along fairly quickly: soon afterwards Ian Mosley took over the drum stool.

Ian, born on June 16, 1953, in Paddington, London, was brought up in a musical atmosphere. He often accompanied his father, a classical solo violinist, to "work", where the young Ian became especially intrigued by percussion playing. He joined the school jazz orchestra, played with several local bands and studied percussion for two years at the Guildhall School Of Music. He played in West End shows like "Hair" and "Jesus Christ Superstar", and belonged at various times to Curved Air, the Gordon Giltrap Band and the Steve Hackett Band. As a session musician, he's been in contact with everyone from Alvin Stardust to Stevie Wonder.

With the line-up stabilised, Marillion went into the Manor Studios, Oxfordshire, with Nick Tauber, to get to work on their second album. "Fugazi" was actually recorded between Manor, Sarm East, Eel Pie and Maison Rouge studios. They only came out of hiding for a mini "Farewell To '83" tour at Hammersmith, Nottingham, Aylesbury, Birmingham and Edinburgh.

The press have been sharply divided in their opinions of Marillion. The "agin them" brigade have been entirely suspicious and reluctant to give any credit where it's due, writing disparagingly of a "progressive rock revival" and always, *always*, dragging in the boring old Genesis comparisons.

Marillion, to their credit, consistently managed to avoid tearing off any journalists' heads, although the whole Genesis spectre did, at times, become an infuriating frustration. If the group had to make their points once, they had to make them several million times.

No, they were not the leaders of any progressive revival; no, there was no such thing as a progressive revival – all Marillion were doing was providing a type of music for which there had always been a demand; no, they would not deny the influences of Genesis, Pink Floyd, Peter Hammill or Yes, but certainly they would like to mention other influences like The Doors, Rush, The Beatles, Elton John, Kate Bush, The Teardrop Explodes, ABC, punk, jazz and folk; no, you can't help absorbing music that's been a soundtrack to your youth and has meant something to you; yes, Marillion are following their own hearts rather than picking anyone else's brains; and, yes, everything that comes from Marillion is their own and it's natural and it's good. So screw you, mate.

The fact that Marillion played long songs with often complex arrangements and poetic language added fuel to the charges against them. Fish would retort that Marillion were aiming for musical value, that the subjects he dealt with in the lyrics would not easily lend themselves to a three-minute dance track, nor could they be covered thoroughly in that short length of time. Furthermore, Marillion, musically and lyrically, were a good deal harder than any of the Seventies bands with whom they were always being compared.

However, the comparisons persisted with dreary predictability, and although they did create a lot of extra press for the group with readers conducting heated debates in the letters pages of the music papers, they also gave rise to two serious problems.

One was the alienation of certain sections of Marillion's potential audience. The fact that they were portrayed as some sort of hippy heavy metal band served to stifle their intentions to reach *everyone*. Secondly, the group felt temporarily "paranoid" of their own material, wary of going ahead with some of their new ideas in case those, too, were judged to sound like *that other band*.

At the same time, Marillion could count on a legion of staunch allies among the press. There were plenty of journalists only too willing to go right over the top about the band, certain of their sincerity, inspired by their versatility and range, and comprehensively entertained by their stagecraft.

Fish has always been a marvellous interviewee (even for the anti-Marillionists), and you only need a couple of days on the road with this band to be convinced of one fact: these are five of the most wonderful men in the world! Oh, they'll give you the serious conversations, the quotable quotes, the soul-searchings until dawn. They're also damned good fun when the mood takes them.

Marillion, after a few grendels, are quite unpredictable. One night, they might be giving firework displays on the beach at midnight, the next they might be ripping the clothes off any unfortunate reporter who happens to fall asleep in their company, the next day again they might be rampaging around German hotel corridors with fire extinguishers.

One party they might rather not have thrown involved a young woman who made Fleet Street headlines after a drinking session with Marillion. She managed to stagger off home with the group's money.

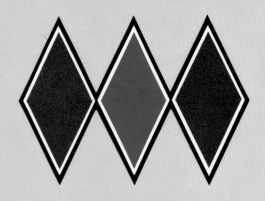

Theatrics have been an integral part of the Marillion set since the earliest days, from Fish's machine-gunning of the crowd during "Forgotten Sons" to a multitude of props which have from time to time included skulls, rubber plants, blood capsules, giant jigsaw pieces and helmets. Fish's spoken introductions to the various compositions are also a revelation.

All of these devices are used to heighten the dramatic impact of the songs, not to distract from them in the slightest. And yet, it should be said that the music, live, is devastating enough to carry the show without any tricks at all, while Fish is a magnetic showman without the costumes... or even the makeup.

Greasepaint originally served a dual purpose: it counteracted Fish's onstage nervousness, the archetypal "mask to hide behind", and it enhanced the impact of his performance. It was only after some time that Fish realised just how effective this mask could be as a theatrical device, with the right facial expression, the right gesture, the right mime, coming together at exactly the same time.

Incidentally, while we're in the Ancient Information Department... if anyone out there is *still* wondering, Fish might drink like one, but his nickname derives from an old Scottish habit of sitting in the bath for hours!

On January 30, 1984, Marillion released another single, the inventive "Punch And Judy" which offered an infectious pop sensibility and an arrangement that highlighted the "punch punch punch" aspects of its subject: wife-battering.

The group followed on with a major British tour in February, incorporating three nights at the Hammersmith Odeon. During that trek, Marillion became the first band to play at a new venue, the Plymouth Skating Rink, on February 26.

The second album, "Fugazi", was in the shops on March 12 as well as a video EP featuring "Grendel" and "The Web", filmed live at Hammersmith the previous April. With the new album, Marillion achieved a tougher, possibly more ambitious sound, with the lead guitar to the fore a little more than in the past.

The theme, this time, related to the state of being "Fugazi" – a word used to mean "all fucked up" by the US

soldiers in Vietnam (Vietnam being a favourite Fish subject). A stirring and complex song, the title track probes the "glitter conscience" as described by Fish: "We've got non-stick frying pans, wonderful new drugs for cancer, micro-chip technology...and yet we've still got slums in Liverpool and Glasgow and everyone ignores them". The lyrics go on to contemplate the dangers of becoming *too* exposed to reality.

"It's like tearing a scab off a wound", says Fish. "You always bleed. You can become nearly totally fugazi. That's when you get to the lines 'Where are the prophets, where are the visionaries, where are the poets?' Someone who can provide me with *some hope*".

Other tracks deal with jealousy ("Emerald Lies"), failed relationships ("Jigsaw"), ruthlessness in friendship ("Assassing"), groupies ("She Chameleon"), and emotional blackmail and uncertainty ("Incubus"). Fish, predictably, has his own unique light to throw on what may seem, superficially, to be well-worn subjects.

"Fugazi", also released as a picture disc, sailed straight up the charts to number five and it was followed, on April 30, by the release of another single, "Assassing" c/w "Cinderella Search". It also came out as a limited edition 12″ picture disc and a conventional 12″ with full-length versions of both tracks. The single made its highest entry at 22.

By then, Marillion were already out of the country, touring Europe, America and Canada. They returned to appear as special guests at Status Quo's last concert at the Milton Keynes Bowl – a performance which won them two encores and a collection of glowing reviews.

In August they were set to headline the three-day "Reading" festival which has been relocated at Lilford Park, Northamptonshire, between August 24 and 26. Unfortunately, the festival was scrapped at the last minute after interference by the local authority on behalf of residents. Fish subsequently lambasted the council as "extreme, ignorant and narrow-minded", and Marillion agreed to make up to disappointed fans by appearing at the Nostell Priory four-day festival near Wakefield, Yorkshire, on August 27. Additionally, they insisted that ticket prices should remain as they were, at £3, before they were added to the bill.

The fact that their hotel, near to the festival site, caught fire while they were in residence had nothing to do with Marillion, we're assured.

Meanwhile, Marillion prepared to release a live album, "Real To Reel", as a direct response to inferior bootleg tapes which changed hands around the country at inflated prices. There had also been requests for a live album from The Web fan club members, and the compilation was furthermore considered a convenient introduction to Marillion in Europe.

Produced by Simon Hanhart and Marillion, the album was released on November 5 at a budget price of around £2.99. The first side, recorded in Montreal, Canada, in June 1984, contained "Assassing", "Incubus" and "Cinderella Search" while the second side, recorded at Leicester De Montfort Hall in March of that year, comprised "Forgotten Sons", "Garden Party" and "Market Square Heroes".

More successful than many live albums, it did maintain a balance between the precision and control of the group's studio work and the atmosphere and power of their live show. However, it didn't carry the excitement of a *new* album, and its sales were not exceptional.

At the time of this release, Marillion played a short series of dates in Britain, flew back to Europe for another tour, and returned to the UK at Christmas for a handful of extra gigs which included another three sold-out nights at the Hammersmith Odeon – making six altogether in 1984.

Fish capped off an exciting year by being voted **Melody Maker's** "Ligger Of The Year" for his outstanding services to hard play as well as hard work, and started off 1985 in high spirits after wangling an interview in **Knave** and a photo session with two **Knave** models and a motor bike.

If Marillion had made mincemeat of their critics by sticking to their guns, carrying on regardless of the sniping, and *succeeding*, then there was bigger and better still to come. 1985 was undoubtedly the year of Marillion. As the new year dawned, they were working on material for the next studio album.

First came the release of a single, "Kayleigh" c/w "Lady Nina" – a song to a prostitute – on April 7. A 12" version, featuring extended performances of both songs, was released on the same date, followed by a seven-inch picture disc a week later. Lyrically, "Kayleigh" was the most explicit and direct song Fish had ever written; musically, its atmospheric simplicity knocked spots off everything else that was kicking round the charts at the time. It soared up to number two and would've made the big one if it hadn't been for the dominance of the charity single, "You'll Never Walk Alone", released in aid of the Bradford City F.C. Fire Disaster fund.

It was Fish's ill-fated love affair with Kayleigh which dominated his emotional excursions on all three albums.

But "Misplaced Childhood", released on June 17 and an immediate number one smash, burns with a huge intensity, assails the listener with all sorts of desperate turmoil from the writer's heart.

Recorded in Berlin's Hansa Ton Studios between March and May 1985 and produced by Chris Kimsey, the album breaks new ground for Marillion in many ways. Most important, it's an unashamed concept album with no breaks between tracks, an idea that not only works but works *brilliantly*, the arrangements crafted to perfection, the melodies intelligently persuasive, the subtleties and textures and tensions painted convincingly, the instruments in balance and intuitively *right* together. This is the album that finally establishes Marillion as a Very Important Force, a band who have fully realised their communal strength, who can give us something very exciting to look forward to in the future.

"Misplaced Childhood" is the most hair-raising document that Fish's notebook has ever produced. At the time of its composition, Fish was struggling with an identity crisis between his "sensible" self, Derek Dick, and his extrovert, walking-the-edge self (Fish). The crisis was exacerbated by the split between him and Kayleigh in October 1983.

"One of the reasons we split", says Fish, "is that I felt I couldn't hold that side together and hold the rock 'n' roll side together. The Fish side assassinated the feelings of Derek so that Fish could carry on".

Instead of recovering from the broken romance, Fish dwelled upon it more and more as the months passed, allowed the Derek/Fish conflict to worsen until he became physically ill with panic attacks. And then came the exorcism in writing, the manuscript that formed the basis of "Misplaced Childhood".

There are two basic ideas at work here, below the wealth of detail on the surface. One is the concept of the wall, the one with which Fish obstructed his relationship with Kayleigh. The other is the idea of "misplaced childhood – the child's voice, Derek's voice, the one I've disregarded for so long". Hence the photograph of 11-year-old Robert Mead on the album cover.

At least, this time, the album has a happy ending. It was long enough coming...

Talking of the three studio albums in retrospect, Fish recently remarked that "'Script' was bedsit thoughts, 'Fugazi' was hotel thoughts and 'Misplaced Childhood' is home thoughts. It heralds the demise of the jester and the introduction of a new character – the child".

It's unusual, however, for Fish to talk at all in terms of separate albums. He sees each Marillion release as a mere part of one greater, living, co-ordinated and integrated whole: the music itself. This, he generally declares, should not be cut up into separate sections for discussion but should be considered rather as a single expanding entity, a continuation of ideas.

You'll find that any one Marillion album will refer and cross-refer to any of the others in symbolism, in lyrical themes and imagery, in musical identity. What the next development will be is anybody's guess. But you can take it from Marillion: "We're sticking to our direction and we're taking a fighting stance". As usual, they mean it.

FISH
SHAMBLES

Discography

✦✦✦ Video Cassettes ✦✦✦

RECITAL OF THE SCRIPT
RELEASED 10.10.83

VIDEO EP ("Grendel" and "The Web")
RELEASED 12.03.84

✦✦✦ Albums ✦ Cassettes ✦✦✦

SCRIPT FOR A JESTER'S TEAR
RELEASED 14.03.83

FUGAZI
RELEASED 12.03.84

REAL TO REEL (Live Album)
(cassette contains bonus track "Emerald Lies")
RELEASED 05.11.84

MISPLACED CHILDHOOD
RELEASED 17.06.85
(*Limited editions of all albums were released as picture discs)

✦✦✦ Singles ✦✦✦

MARKET SQUARE HEROES/Three Boats Down From The Candy
12" features "Grendel"
RELEASED 25.10.82

HE KNOWS, YOU KNOW/Charting The Single
12" features full-length album version of A-side
RELEASED 31.01.83

GARDEN PARTY/Margaret
12" features a full length "Garden Party", a 13-minute "Margaret"
and a live version of "Charting The Single"
RELEASED 06.06.83

PUNCH AND JUDY/
Market Square Heroes/Three Boats Down From The Candy
the latter two both re-recorded
RELEASED 30.01.84

ASSASSING/Cinderella Search
Also comes in 12" picture disc and conventional 12"
which has full-length versions of both tracks
RELEASED 30.04.84

KAYLEIGH/Lady Nina
The 12" features extended mixes of both tracks
RELEASED 07.04.85
7" picture disc released a week later
RELEASED 13.04.85